PYTHON FOR DATA ANALYSIS

A PRACTICAL GUIDE YOU CAN'T
MISS TO MASTER DATA USING
PYTHON. KEY TOOLS FOR DATA
SCIENCE, INTRODUCING YOU INTO
DATA MANIPULATION, DATA
VISUALIZATION, MACHINE
LEARNING.

ERICK THOMPSON

TABLE OF CONTENTS

INTRODUCTION

Data analysis plays an important part in many aspects of life today. A lot of important decisions are made based on data analytics. Companies need data to help them meet many of their goals. As the population of the world keeps growing, its customer base keeps expanding. In light of this, they must find ways of keeping their customers happy while at the same time meeting their business goals.

Given the nature of competition in the business world, it is not easy to keep customers happy. Competitors keep preying on each other's customers, and those who win have another challenge ahead - how to maintain the customers lest they slide back to their former business partners. This is one area where Data Analysis comes in handy.

To understand their customers better, companies rely on data. They collect all manner of data at each point of interaction with their customers. Data are useful in several ways. The companies learn more about their customers, thereafter clustering them according to their specific needs. Through such segmentation, the company can attend to the customers' needs better and hope to keep them satisfied for longer.

But, data analytics is not just about customers and the profit motive. It is also about governance. Governments are the biggest data consumers all over the world. They collect data about citizens, businesses, and every other entity that they interact with at any given point. This is important information because it helps in a lot of instances.

For planning purposes, governments need accurate data on their population so that funds can be allocated accordingly. Equitable distribution of resources is something that cannot be achieved without proper Data Analysis. Other than planning, there is also the security angle. To protect the country, the government must maintain different databases for different reasons. There are high profile individuals who must be accorded special security detail, top threats who must be monitored at all times, and so forth. To meet the security objective, the government has to obtain and maintain updated data on persons of interest at all times.

There is so much more to Data Analysis than corporate and government decisions. As a programmer, you are

venturing into an industry that is challenging and exciting at the same time. Data doesn't lie unless it is manipulated, in which case you need insane Data Analysis and handling skills. As a data analyst, you will come across many challenges and problems that need solutions that can only be handled through Data Analysis. The way you interact with data can make a big difference, bigger than you can imagine.

There are several equipments you can use for Data Analysis. Many people use Microsoft Excel for Data Analysis and it works well for them. However, there are limitations of using Excel which you can overcome through Python. Learning Python is a good initiative, given that it is one of the easiest programming languages. It is a high-level programming language because its syntax is so close to the normal language we use.

For expert programmers, you have gone beyond learning about the basics of Python and graduated into using Python to solve real-world problems. Many problems can be solved through Data Analysis. The first challenge is usually understanding the issue at hand, then working on a data solution for it.

Knowledge of Python libraries is indeed important. It is by understanding these libraries that you can go on to become an expert data analyst with Python.

As you interact with data, you do understand the importance of cleaning data to ensure the outcome of your analysis is not flawed. You will learn how to go about this and build on that to make sure your work is perfect. Another challenge that many organizations have is protecting the integrity of data. You should try and protect your organization from using contaminated data. There are procedures you can make use of to make sure that you use clean data all the time.

Data is produced and stored in large amounts daily from automated systems. Learning Data Analysis through Python should help you process and extract information from data and make meaningful conclusions from them. One area where these skills will come in handy is forecasting. Through Data Analysis, you can create predictive models that should help your organization meet its objectives.

A good predictive model is only near as good as the quality of data introduced into it, the data modeling methods, and more importantly, the dataset used for the analysis. Beyond data handling and processing, one other important aspect of Data Analysis is visualization. Visualization is about presentation. Your data model should be good enough for an audience to read and understand it at the first point of contact. Apart from the audience, you should also learn how to plot data on different visualizations to help you get an irregular idea of the nature of the data you are working with.

When you are done with Data Analysis, you should have a data model complete with visual concepts that will help in predicting outcomes and responses before you can proceed to the testing phase. Data analysis is a study that is currently in high demand in different fields. Knowing what to do, as well as when and how to handle data, is an important skill that you should not take lightly. Through this, you can build and test a hypothesis and go on to understand systems better.

CHAPTER - 1

INTRODUCTION TO PYTHON AND

DATA ANALYSIS

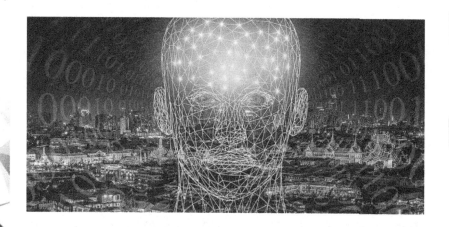

Data Science and Data Analysis

The words of data science and data analytics are often used interchangeably. However, these terms are completely different and have different implications for different businesses. Data science encompasses a variety of scientific models and methods that can be used to manipulate and survey structured, semi structured, and unstructured data. Tools and processes that can be used to make sense of gather insight from highly complex, unorganized and raw data set falls under the category of data science. Unlike data analytics that is targeted to verify a hypothesis, data science boils down to connecting data points to identify new patterns and insights that can be made use of in future planning for the business. Data science moves the business from inquiry to insights by providing a new perspective into their structured and unstructured data by identifying patterns that can allow businesses to increase efficiencies, reduce costs and recognize the new market opportunities.

Data science acts as a multidisciplinary blend of technology, machine learning algorithm development, statistical analysis, and data inference that provides businesses with enhanced capability to solve their most complex business problems. Data analytics falls under the category of data science and pertains more to reviewing and analyzing historical data to put it in context. Unlike data science, data analytics is characterized by low usage of artificial intelligence, predictive modeling and machine learning algorithms to gather insights from processed and structured data using standard SQL query commands. The seemingly nuanced differences between data analytics and data science can actually have a substantial impact on an organization.

Python as top languages for developers at top companies

When startups are planning a process of product development, they need to keep in mind and take note of different factors when it comes to choosing the right language for programming. Moreover, since many startups start from scratch, the budget available is often low, and this is why they very carefully consider factors like how swift the development would be, how popular and widely use the language is factors like the cost of libraries, integrations, and developers. In addition, the cost of security and scalability and not to forget stability. Due to these reasons, it is always preferred by startups around the world and especially in Silicon Valley to opt for a robust and strong technology like Python, which is established and deep-rooted.

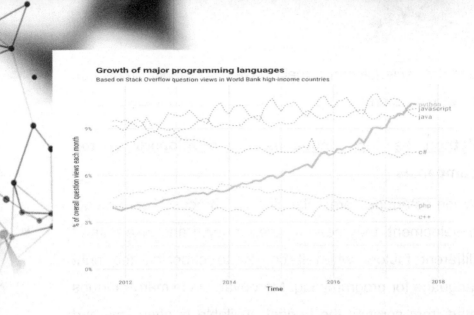

Growth of major programming languages
Based on Stack Overflow question views in World Bank high-income countries

This is not the start of technology. It has been around for more than as long as 30 years in the market, and it is so robust and established that it is still one of the tops and best languages for programming that ever existed. This means that Python is so established and widely used that even the latest innovations in the IT sector could not elbow it aside. According to a survey by BuiltWith, as many as one million websites out there are Python costumers and have been performing pretty amazingly with great returns. Credit goes to the robust programing language. Another survey about the popularity of Python by TIOBE INDEX reveals that an index called programming community index PCI that measures how popular the programing languages are has ranked Python as the third most famous and popular programing language around the world.

Python for Data Analysis

Python is among the most popular computer language programming tool initially created and designed by Guido Van Rossum in the late 1980s. Since its introduction into the computing world, Python has undergone multiple modifications and improvements, therefore, becoming among leading programming languages used by developers. The tool is dynamically typed, object-oriented, multi-paradigm, and imperative. It is used across different operating systems including Windows, Linux, Android, macOS, and iOS devices. Besides, it is compatible with both bit 32 and bit 64 gadgets of phones, laptops, and desktops.

Despite comprising of several areas essential for programmers, Python is easy to learn, especially when it comes to beginners with minimal knowledge in computer programming. Unlike most programming languages, Python accompanies an easy to use syntaxes where first time users can readily practice and become a pro within a few weeks. However, the programming processes may vary depending on the motive of the learner in programming. Despite accompanying multiple vocabularies and sometimes sophisticated tutorials for learning different programming techniques, engaging with Python is worth it to develop excellent programs.

CHAPTER - 2

PYTHON BASICS

N ow that we have look at Python and some of the benefits that come with it to ensure we get the full reasons why someone would want to use it for data analysis, it is time for us to go through some of the basics of writing code in Python. There are a lot of different parts that are all going to come together to help us make sure that we are writing our codes out well, and that we actually learn what Python is all about.

Python history

Python programming began at the fingertips of a Dutch programmer, name of Guido Van Rossum. He wrote the program sometime in the latter period of the '80s as a hobby project. Since its release to the public, Python has grown and evolved over time to be one of the most acclaimed, polished, and consistent languages in the world of computer programming.

According to Van Rossum, the conception of Python can be traced to a Christmas weekend in December 1989. He had begun working on his hobby project in his free time to develop an interpreter language—a successor to the ABC programming language to which Van Rossum helped develop. However, when the entire process of development came to an end, Python emerged as nothing short of a complete programming language in itself. Given its somewhat already weird history, the name "Python" draws even more questions to the identity of the programming language. Van Rossum had the Unix and C hackers as the target audience of his program, but more importantly, he was especially keen on the then famous TV sitcom—The Monty Python's Flying Circus. Van Rossum explained that he found the name "Python" not only suitable to his taste but appealing to his target audience, so he ran with it.

Installing Python

To install Python, visit https://www.python.org/. Navigate to the Downloads field where you'll proceed to download the latest Python version depending on your Operating system.

Python Comments

The next thing that we need to take a look at in the comments. These are going to be unique parts of any code that allow you to add in a little bit of a note or information into the code without it actually affecting the code or causing it to have an error.

If you would like to name a certain part of the code, or you want to leave a little message for yourself, or for another programmer who would take a look through your information and your code. You can explain what is going through that part of the code for yourself or someone else, get it a different name, or something else.

Working on the comments is going to be simple to work with. Each code is going to work with these comments in a slightly different manner, but in the Python language, we just need to use the # symbol ahead of the comment. You can have the comment be as long or short as you would like, and you can have as many of these in your code as you would like as well. The rule is to just keep this to a minimum as much as possible, though, to ensure the code stays nice and clean along the way.

Numbers

Numbers are a type of data type used to store numeric values only. Python supports three types of numbers. They include floats, integers, and complex numbers.

Unlike some programming languages where you declare the variable data type before using it, Python requires you to only declare the name of the variable, and then the equal sign and the assigned value.

```
age = 22
```

Floats

We use floats, also called real-numbers, to represent decimal numbers, and we frequently represent them with a decimal point. In Python, we can also represent floats in scientific notation using the exponential symbol. Example: 0.84e5 = 84000.0

Integers

In Python, we use Integers to represent 'whole' numerical values that do not have decimal points. Integers can be either positive or negative representation.

```
x = 10
y = -34
type(x)
type(y)
```

```
int
```

Complex Numbers

In python, we represent Complex numbers as x + yi where x and y represent float numbers, and i equals the square root of -1 (imaginary number). Complex numbers are not very common in Python programming but the language does support them.

Long

Long, also called long integers, are integers of unlimited size. We write them as integers followed by uppercase or lowercase L. Only Python2 supports this type of numbers.

To find the type of a variable, use the type() method built into python

Lists

Another topic that is going to show up when we work with Python is the differences between a list and a dictionary, and even a tuple. First, we are going to explore what the lists are like. The list is going to actually have the most versatility when it comes to types of objects that are used in Python. Some of the things that we will notice when working on these lists include

1. A list is going to be an ordered and mutable sequence of items. Because of this, it is something that we are able to slice, index, and change along the way. Each element is something that we are able to access using the position it has on the list. Python lists are going to work for most of the collection data structures, and since they are found as built-in, you do not have to go through the process of manually creating them.

2. Lists are going to be used for any object type, from strings to numbers and to more lists as well.

3. They are going to be accessed just like a string, which means that they are simple to use, and they will be variable in length. We are able to see them shrink and grow automatically as we use them.

4. List variables are going to be declared when we work with the brackets, and then the name of the variable will be ahead of it.

Tuples

Another option to explore is known as a tuple. Tuples are going to be used in Python to help hold together more than one object. Think of this as something that is similar to the list, but it is not going to have the extensive functionality that the list class is going to provide to us. One of the major features that we will like about these tuples is that they are going to be immutable, similar to strings, which means we are not able to modify them.

Even though modification is not allowed here, you are able to take portions of some of the existing tuples and use it to make a new tuple. Lists are going to be declared with a square bracket, and then we are able to change them as needed. However, the tuple is going to be found in the parentheses, and we are not able to change them at all.

Dictionaries

A dictionary is much like an address book. If you know the name of the person you wish to contact, you can obtain the details of that person. The name of the person is the key, while the details of the person are the value.

The key that you use in a dictionary should be an immutable data type; that is, it can be a number, tuple, or string. The value can be anything. A dictionary is a mutable data type, and it is for this reason that you can add, modify or remove any pairs from the dictionary. The keys are mapped to an object, and it is for this reason that a dictionary is also known as mappings. This will show you that a dictionary behaves differently to a sequence.

A dictionary can be used anywhere you want to store a value or attribute that will describe an entity or a concept. For instance, you can use a dictionary to count the number of instances of a specific state or object. Since every key has a unique identifier, you cannot have duplicate values for the same key. Therefore, the key can be used to store the items in the input data, and the values can store the result of the calculation.

Python Function

Now that we have a better idea of how the classes are going to work in Python and why these are so important to some of the work that we want to create in this language, it is time to move on to some of the other parts of coding that are important for our goals as well. In particular, we are going to spend a bit of time looking at the steps that we are able to follow in order to create a function in the Python language.

A function, to start with, is just going to be a block of code, any block of code, which is only going to run when the compiler calls it out. You are able to pass on data, which will be known as a parameter, over to your function to ensure that it is going to work in the manner that you want. And then, as the function continues to do its job, it is able to return data as a result as well.

With this in mind, we need to take a look at some of the steps that we are able to use in order to create and then call one of the functions that we want to work with. This is fairly simple because we are able to define one of these functions with the use of the def keyword. The code that you can use to create one of these functions includes:

def my_function():

print("Hello from a function")

The code that we will focus on here is going to have a function that just has one argument, which is known as (fname) when we are able to call up the function, we will pass along the first name, which is the going to be used inside of the function to help us get the full name printed off as well.

Now that we have brought up both the idea of a parameter and that of an argument, we need to figure out which one is going to be the best one to use for our codes. The terms of argument and parameter can be used for the same thing because both of them are going to include information that is passed on over to the function.

When we look at this from the perspective of the function, the parameter is going to be a variable that is listed inside of the parentheses in the definition of the function. The argument, on the other hand, is going to be the value that has been sent to the function when it is called out. We can use both in a similar manner along the way, though.

We can also work with the idea that is known as recursion. Python is also going to accept what is known as function recursion, which means that the defined function is able to come through and call itself.

Recursion is going to be a common concept in programming and mathematics. It means that a function is going to call itself. This has the benefit of allowing programming to loop through the data to reach the result that we are working with.

If you want to work with recursion, you need to be careful with the work that you handle here. It is easy to mess up and start writing a function that is never going to terminate, or one that is going to use too much memory or processing power to get the work done. However, when it is written out in the correct manner, it is possible for recursion to be efficient, and an elegant approach, mathematically, when you do your programming.

Strings

Now it is time to take a look at something that is known as the Python strings. We did take a look at these a bit with some of the other topics, but now it is time to give them a look of their own. To make this process simple, remember that this string is going to just be a series of text characters that are found in your code and can help you to get things done.

There are a few different operators that we need to focus on when we want to handle our strings in Python. An operator is going to be a simple symbol that we are able to use to perform the operations that are necessary inside of our code. Some of the operators that we need to spend the most time looking through when we work with Python include:

- Concatenation operator: This is the operator that you would want to use when it is time to concatenate strings.

- Repetition operator: This is the operator that you will use in order to create many copies of a string. You can choose how many times you would like to repeat the string.

- Slice operator: This is the operator that is going to look through your string and then retrieve the specific character that you want from there. Any time that you use this one, you would need to remember that zero is going to be the first character of the string.

- Range slice operator: This is the operator that is going to retrieve a range of characters from your index, rather than just one character. If you just want to showcase one word or one part of your string, you would use this kind of operator.

- In operator: This operator is going to search for a specified character in a target string. If the character is present somewhere in the string, then you will get an answer of True returned to you. If that character is not inside the string, then you will get an answer of False returned to you.

- No in operator: This is the operator that will work in the opposite manner as the in operator. It is going to search for a specified character in your string. But if the operator is not able to find that character in the string, then you will get the True answer returned. If that character is found in the string, then it is going to return False.

Boolean

Python Boolean is a data type that contains only two number diagrams. Both values generally represent true or false, which is logical or boolean algebra. In most cases, the two qualities in Boolean algebra are generally consistent. Contingent upon how Boolean impacts or portrays a circumstance, restrictive proclamations are related to activities on how the designer chooses. In this, the value represented by logic does not necessarily have to be Boolean.

Loop

There are actually a few different types of loops that we are able to work with when it comes to Python. These are going to be nice because they take out some of the work. If there is a part of the code that you would like to see repeat itself a bunch of times, rather than rewriting out that part of code over and over again, we would simply turn it into a loop. In specific, we are going to take a look at what the loop is about and how we can utilize this for our needs too.

To start, the loop is going to be used to help us iterate over one of the sequences that we want to use. This could be a string, a set, a dictionary, a tuple, or a list. This is going to be less like the keyword that we see with other coding languages, and it is more like the iterator method for other OOP languages.

When we focus on the loop, we are going to spend some time executing a set of specific statements that we want to see taken care of. This is going to happen one time for each item on the list, tuple, or set. A good example that we can look at here is below:

```
fruits = ["apple", "banana", "cherry"]

for x in fruits:

print(x)
```

Now in some cases, we also have to make sure that we add in a break statement. This will ensure that the code will know where to stop and that it is not going to keep going in an endless loop that we are not able to stop. This will effectively freeze up our computers and make it hard to work with them without exiting the whole program. Set up the broken part in this to ensure that it will behave in the manner that you want.

CHAPTER - 3

ESSENTIAL PYTHON LIBRARIES AND

INSTALLATION

What is Matplotlib?

There are a lot of different libraries that we are able to work with when it is time to handle visuals and other work of data analysis inside of our Python language. But the library that we are going to spend some time taking a look at is one that is meant to work with the idea of data visualization and why this is so important to some of the work that we want to accomplish.

To start with, you will find that matplotlib is going to be a plotting library that is set up to work with Python. It is also going to be a numerical mathematics extension that works off the arrays that we see in NumPy. This means that if we want to work with the matplotlib library, we need to first make sure that we have NumPy, and sometimes other libraries as well, on our system and ready to go as well.

When we are working with Matplotlib, you will find that it is useful when it is time to provide an API that is object-oriented for embedding plots into applications that will work with some of the toolkits for GUI that is general-purpose. There is also going to be a procedural interface based on a state machine that will work similar to MATLAB, although these are both going to be completely different things from one another, and it is important to work with them in a different manner.

The matplotlib is a great library to work with, and it was originally written by John D. Hunter. It is also going to impress a lot of new programmers because it has a development community that is active. It is also going to be distributed with a license that is BSD so that it is easier for us to use the way that we would like overall.

There are a lot of really cool options that you are able to work with when it is time to handle the matplotlib library, and this opens up a lot of opportunities for you when it is time to pick out the different choices in visuals. There are many of these that you are able to work with, and thanks to the way that matplotlib is set up, you will be able to pick out almost any kind of visual that you would like to work with as well.

This means that if you want to make a chart, a pie graph, a bar graph, a histogram, or some other kind of chart, this library is going to have a lot of the additional parts that we are looking for when it is time to handle your data. Make sure to take a look at some of the different options that are provided with this library, and then pay attention to what we are able to do with them before picking the one that is the best for you.

There are also going to be a number of different toolkits that you are able to handle when it is time to work with Matplotlib. These toolkits are important because they are going to help us to really extend out the amount of functionality that we will see with this library. Depending on the one that you would like to work with, some of them are going to be separate kinds of downloads, and some are going to ship along with the source code that is found in this library, but their dependencies are going to be found outside of this library, so we have to pay attention to this as well. Some of the different toolkits that we are able to work with include:

1. The basemap: This is going to be a map plotting tool that we are able to use to help out with different types of projects of a map, coastlines, and political boundaries that we are going to see in here.

2. Cartopy: This is another good one to work with when it is time to handle maps and some of that kind of work. This is going to be a mapping library that will have object-oriented map project definitions and arbitrary point lines, image transformation, and even polygon capabilities as well.

3. This one can also come with a number of Excel tools if you would like to work with these as well. This makes it easier for us to use Excel as our database, and you will easily be able to set this up so that you are able to exchange data from your matplotlib library and Excel.

4. GTK tools that are going to allow us the ability to interface and work with the GTK+ library if you would like.

5. The Qt interface.

6. The ability to work with 3-D plots to help out with some of the visuals that you are going to want to use along the way.

7. Natgrid: This is going to be an interface that will allow us into the library of natgrid for gridding irregularly spaced data when you would like.

There are a few other libraries that help with visuals if you would like, but we have to remember that this is one of the best ones to work with, and they will keep things as simple and easy to use as possible. And with all of the added and nice features that are going to come with this, you will be able to see some great results with your visuals as well.

Statsmodel

Statsmodel is another Python library for data science widely used for statistical analysis. Statsmodel is a Python library used to perform statistical tests and implement various statistical models for extensive data exploration. Statsmodel was developed at Stanford University by Professor Jonathan Taylor. Compared with Scikit-learn, statsmodel has algorithms for classical statistics and econometrics.

They include submodules such as:

- Regression models such as linear mixed-effects models, robust linear models, generalized linear models and linear regression.

- Nonparametric methods such as Kernel density estimation and kernel regression.

- Analysis of variance.

- Time series analysis

- Visualization of statistical model results

SciPy

What's SciPy for?

Python customers who prefer a quick and effective math library can use NumPy, however NumPy through itself isn't very task-focused.

How SciPy 1.0 helps with data science

SciPy has always been beneficial for supplying handy and extensively used equipment for working with math and statistics.

The set off for bringing the SciPy challenge to model 1.0, in accordance with core developer Ralf Gommers, used to be specifically a consolidation of how the mission once ran and managed. But it additionally covered a procedure for non-stop integration for the MacOS and Windows builds, as nicely as a suitable aid for prebuilt Windows binaries. This ultimate characteristic ability Windows customers can now use SciPy by not having to soar through extra hoops.

Where to obtain SciPy?

SciPy binaries can be gotten from the Python Package Index, or via typing pip installation scipy. Source code is reachable on GitHub.

Pandas

Pandas are going to be a big name when we want to use the Python language to analyze the data we have, and it is actually one of the most used tools that we can bring out when it comes to data wrangling and data munging. Pandas are open-sourced, similar to what we see with some of the other libraries and extensions that are found in Python world. It is also free to use and will be able to handle all of the different parts of your data analysis.

There is a lot that you will enjoy when working with the Pandas library, but one of the neat things is that this library is able to take data, of almost any format that you would like, and then create a Python object out of it. This is known as a data frame and will have the rows and columns that you need to keep it organized. It is going to look similar to what we are used to seeing with an Excel sheet.

To start with, we are going to use this library to help us to load and save our data. When you want to use this particular library to help out with data analysis, you will find that you can use it in three different manners. These include:

1. You can use it to convert a Python dictionary or list, or aa array in NumPy to a data frame with the help of this library.

2. You can use it to open up a local file with Pandas. This is usually going to be done in a CSV file, but it is also possible to do it in other options like a delimited text file or in Excel.

3. You can also open a remote file or a database like JSON or CSV on one of the websites through a URL, or you can use it to read out the information that is found on an SQL table or database.

Numpy

NumPy is the key bundle for logical registering in Python. It is a Python library that offers a multidimensional showcase object, unique inferred objects, (for example, veiled clusters and grids), and a grouping of schedules for rapid tasks on clusters, consisting of numerical, coherent, structure control, arranging, choosing, I/O, discrete Fourier changes, quintessential straight variable based math, indispensable factual activities, irregular reenactment and substantially more.

At the center of the NumPy bundle, is the ndarray object. This exemplifies n-dimensional varieties of homogeneous information types, with numerous activities being carried out in assembling code for execution. There are a few significant contrasts between NumPy well-known shows and the popular Python groupings:

- NumPy clusters have a constant measurement at creation, distinctive to Python documents (which can advance progressive). Changing the measurement of a ndarray will make some other exhibit and erase the first.

- The aspects in a NumPy cluster are altogether required to be of comparable data type, and in consequence will be a comparative dimension in memory. The unique case: one can have the sorts of (Python, inclusive of NumPy) objects, alongside these strains taking into account sorts of quite a number estimated components.

- NumPy reveals encourage stepped forward numerical and one of a kind kinds of things to do on massive portions of information. Ordinarily, such duties are carried out more productively and with much less code than is conceivable utilizing Python's worked in successions.

- Creating lots of logical and scientific Python-based bundles are making use of NumPy exhibits; however these in most cases bolsters Python-succession input, they convert such contribution to NumPy clusters earlier than preparing, and they frequently yield NumPy clusters. At the end of the day, so as to efficaciously utilize a great deal (maybe even most) of the present logical/scientific Python-based programming, truly realizing how to make use of Python's labored in succession kinds is missing - one likewise has to realize how to utilize NumPy exhibits.

The focus on grouping size and velocity is particularly widespread in logical registering. As a fundamental model, consider the instance of growing each and every aspect in a 1-D grouping with the referring to issue in another succession of a comparable length. In the match that the statistics are put away in two Python records, an and b, we should emphasize each component:

This creates the proper answer, but on the off chance that an and b each comprise a massive number of numbers, we will pay the price for the wasteful elements of circling in Python. We ought to reap a comparable assignment substantially extra swiftly in C by means of composing (for lucidity we disregard variable displays and instatements, memory designation, and so forth.)

This spares all the overhead engaged with interpreting the Python code and controlling Python objects, yet to the detriment of the advantages picked up from coding in Python. Moreover, the coding work required increments with the dimensionality of our information. On account of a 2-D cluster, for instance, the C code (abbreviated as in the past) grows to NumPy offers us the quality of the two universes: thing by-component things to do are the "default mode" when an ndarray is included, but the aspect by-component undertaking is swiftly carried out with the aid of pre-gathered C code. In NumPy

```
c = a * b
```

Does what the preceding fashions do, at shut C speeds, but with the code effortlessness we count on from something dependent on Python. Surely, the NumPy phrase is lots less complex! This last mannequin represents two of NumPy's highlights which are the premise of a lot of its capacity: vectorization and broadcasting.

Vectorization depicts the non appearance of any unequivocal circling, ordering, and so forth., in the code - these matters are occurring, obviously, honestly "in the background" in advanced, pre-incorporated C code. Vectorized code has numerous preferences, among which are:

- vectorized code is steadily brief and less difficult to peruse
- fewer lines of code for the most section implies fewer bugs
- the code all the extra closely takes after well-known numerical documentation (making it simpler, commonly, to precise code scientific develops)
- vectorization brings about greater "Pythonic" code. Without vectorization, our code would be covered with wasteful and tough to peruse for circles.

Broadcasting is the term used to depict the sore issue by-component behavior of activities; for the most section talking, in NumPy all tasks, wide variety juggling tasks, yet coherent, piece shrewd, utilitarian, and so forth., elevate on in this verifiable factor by-component design, i.e., they communicate. Besides, in the model over, an and bought to be multidimensional types of a comparable shape, or a scalar and an exhibit, or even two sorts of with a variety of shapes, gave that the little cluster is "expandable" to the kingdom of the higher so that the subsequent talk is unambiguous. For factor by way of point "rules" of broadcasting see numpy.doc.broadcasting.

Scikit-Learn

You are not going to get too far when it comes to working on a data analysis if you do not bring in the Scikit-Learn library. This is going to be seen as one of the simple and efficient tools that you can use for data mining and for completing data analysis. What is so great about this one is that it is going to be accessible to anyone, and it can be reusable in many contexts as well. It is also going to come to us with a commercially usable license and it is open source, so we are able to work with it and use it in the manner that we want. Some of the features that we are likely to see with this one include:

1. It can help with problems of classification. This is where it helps us to identify which category a particular object is going to belong with.

2. It can help with some problems of regression. This is where it is able to predict a continuous value attribute associated with the object.

3. It can help with some problems with clustering. This is where we are going to have an automatic grouping of objects that are similar in the sets.

4. It can help us complete something that is known as dimensionality reduction. This is where we are able to

reduce the number of random variables that we want to normalize in all of this.

IPython

Another environment that we can look at is the IPython environment. This is a bit different from some of the others, but it is going to help us to get some more work done. IPython is going to be a shell that is interactive and works well with the Python programming language. It is there to help us to work with many good source codes and can do some tab completion, work with some additional shell syntax, and enhanced introspection all on one.

This is going to be one of the alternatives that we can get with the Python interpreter. A shell is more interactive that can be used for some of the computing that you want to do in Python. In addition, it can provide us with more features based on what we would like to do with our work.

You can enjoy several features when working on the IPython environment. First, it will help you to run more shell commands that are native. When you run any of the interpreters that you would like to use, the interpreter should have a number of commands that are built-in. These commands are sometimes going to collide with the native commands of the shell.

For example, if we wanted to work with the traditional interpreter of Python and we typed in the code of "cd" after the interpreter loaded up, you would get an error on your screen. The reason for this error is that the interpreter is not going to recognize this command. This is a command that is native to the terminal of your computer, but not to the Python interpreter. On the other hand, IPython is going to have some more support for those native shell commands so you can utilize them in your work.

IPython is also a good one to work with when it comes to syntax highlighting. One of the first things that we are going to notice about this is that it provides us with syntax highlighting. This means that it is going to use color to help us look over the different parts of the Python code. If you type in x = 10 to your terminal, you would be able to see how the IPython environment is going to highlight this code in a variety of colors. The syntax highlighting is going to be a big improvement over what we see in the default interpreter of Python and can help us to read the code a bit better.

Another benefit of working with IPython is that it works with the proper indentation to help you out. If you have done some coding in the past, you know that it does pay attention to the indentation and whitespace. IPython recognizes this and then automatically provides you with the right indentation as you type the code into this interpreter. This makes things a lot easier as you go through the process.

This environment is also going to work with tab completion. IPython is going to provide us with some tab-completion so that we do not have to worry about handling this. This helps to ensure that the compiler is going to know what is going on with the codes that we write and that all of the work will show up in the manner that you want.

Documentation is another feature that we are able to see with IPython, and it is going to help us to work well with the code. Doing the autocompletion of tabs is going to be useful because it will provide us with a list of all the methods that are possible inside of the specific module. With all of the options at your disposal, you may be confused at what one particular method does. In addition, this is where the documentation of IPython can come into play. It will provide you with the documentation for any method you work with to save time and hassle.

Then the final benefit that we are going to look at here is that IPython can help with pasting blocks of code. IPython is going to be excellent when we want to paste large amounts of Python code. You can grab any block of the

Python code, paste it into this environment, and you should get the result of a code that is properly indented and ready to go on this environment. It is as easy as all that.

You can choose to work with the regular Python environment if you would like, but there are also many benefits to upgrading and working with this one as well, especially when you are working with something like data science and completing your own data analysis.

CHAPTER - 4

IPYTHON AND JUPITER

IPython

IPython same as Interactive Python is a capable toolkit that allows you to experience Python interactively. It has two main components: a dependent Python Shell interface, and Jupyter kernels.

These components have many features, such as:

Persistent input history

Caching of outputs

Code completition

Support for 'magic' commands

Highly customizable settings

Syntax highlighting

Session logging

Access to system Shell

Support for python's debugger and profiler

Now, let's go into each of these components and see how these features come to life.

IPython Shell

The objective of this Shell is to provide a superior experience than the default Python REPL.

To run the IPython Shell you just need to call the command bellow on your system console.

§ Interface

At first glance, the IPython Shell looks like a normal boring Shell, some initial version information and some user tips. However, it has great features that make it shine.

§ Help

You can type "?" after an accessible object at any time you want more details about it.

§ Code Completition

You can press "TAB" key at any time to trigger the code completition.

§ Syntax Highlight

The code is automatically highlighted depending on the variables and keywords you are using.

§ Run External Commands

External commands can be run directly using "!" at the beginning of the input.

§ Magic Commands

Magic commands add incredible capabilities to IPython. Some commands are shown bellow:

%time – Shows the time to execute the command.

%timeit – Shows the mean and standard deviation of the time to execute the command.

%pdb – Run the code in debug mode, creating breakpoints on uncaught exceptions.

%matplotlib – This command arranges all the setup needed to IPython work correctly with matplotlib, this way IPython can display plots that are outputs of running code in new windows.

There are multiple magic commands that be used on IPython Shell, for a full list of the built-in commands check this link or type "%lsmagic".

Jupiter Notebook

Getting started with Jupyter Notebook (IPython)

The Jupyter Note pad is an open-source web application that permits you to produce and share files that contain live code, formulas, visualizations and narrative text. Utilizes consist of information cleansing and change, mathematical simulation, analytical modeling, information visualization, artificial intelligence, and far more.

Jupyter has assistance for over 40 various shows languages and Python is among them. Python is a requirement (Python 3.3 or higher, or Python 2.7) for setting up the Jupyter Notebook itself.

Setting up Jupyter utilizing Anaconda

Set up Python and Jupyter utilizing the Anaconda Distribution, which includes Python, the Jupyter Notebook, and other typically utilized bundles for clinical computing and information science. You can download Anaconda's newest Python3 variation.

Command to run the Jupyter notebook:

When the Notepad opens in your Internet browser, you will see the Notebook Dashboard, which will reveal a list of the notepads, files, and subdirectories in the directory site where the Notepad server was started. Most of the time, you will want to begin a Notepad server in the greatest level directory site consisting of notepads. Typically, this will be your house directory site.

CHAPTER - 5

NUMPY FOR NUMERICAL DATA PROCESSING

Object ndarray

An ndarray object is an n-dimensional structure that stores data. Only one type of data is stored in a ndarray. We can have ndarray objects with as many dimensions as necessary (a dimension for a vector, two dimensions for a matrix ...).

Ndarray objects are a "minimal" format for storing data. Ndarray objects have specific optimized methods that allow you to do calculations extremely fast. It is possible to store ndarray in files to reduce the necessary resources. The ndarray has two important attributes: the type and the shape. When creating a ndarray, we can define the type and the shape or let Python infer these values.

To use NumPy, we always use the same method: import numpy as np. From now on, we use the term array to designate a ndarray object.

Building An Array

The easiest way to build an array is to use the function of

```
NumPy: np.array ()
```

We can create an array from a list with:

```
array_de_liste np.array = ([1,4,7,9])
```

This function takes other parameters including the type, that is to say, the typical elements of the array. The types are very varied in NumPy. Outside of classical types such as int, float, boolean or str, there are many types in NumPy. We will come back to this in the next paragraph.

We can create an array from a series of numbers with the function range () which works like the Python range () function.

```
In []: array_range = np.arange (10)

print (array_range)

[0123456789]
```

Apart from the arrange () function of NumPy, we can use the linspace () function which will return numbers in an interval with a constant distance from one to the other:

```
In []: array_linspace = np.linspace (0,9,10) print (array_linspace)
```

We see that 0 is the lower bound, 9 is the upper bound and we divide into 10 values. We can specify each time the dtype = in each function. From specific formats, there are functions to generate arrays.

Creating and modify Arrays

The development of Python-related data has mostly been done thanks to a package absolutely central for Python. This is NumPy (an abbreviation of Numerical Python). NumPy makes it possible to transform a very classical programming language in a numerical oriented language. It has been developed and improved for many years and now offers an extremely well-organized system of data management.

The central element of NumPy is the array that stores values in a structure supporting all types of advanced calculations. The strength of NumPy lies largely in the fact that it is not coded directly in Python but in C, which gives it an unequaled processing speed with the "classic" Python code. The goal of the NumPy developers is to provide a simple, fast and comprehensive tool to support the various developments in the field of digital processing. NumPy is often presented at the same time as SciPy, a package for scientific computing based on structure from NumPy.

NumPy is useful for both novice and seasoned developers seasoned. ndarray, which are n-dimensional structures, are used by all Python users to process the data. Moreover, the tools allowing to interface Python with other languages such as C or Fortran are not used only by more advanced developers.

Broadcasting

The notion of broadcasting is linked to the fact of managing vector computations on arrays of various sizes. NumPy allows you to do calculations on arrays with different sizes. The simplest rule is:

Two dimensions are compatible when they are equal or if one of the two is of dimension 1. Broadcasting is a way of extending large arrays to adapt them to operations on operators with larger dimensions.

Examples of broadcasting:

If you have two arrays built as follows:

```
In []: arr1 = np.array ([1,4,7,9])

arr2 = np.ones (3)

arr1 + arr2

shapes (4,) (3,)

In []: arr3 = np.ones ((3,4))

arr1 + OFF3

Out []: array ([[2,5,8,10],

[2,5,8,10]

[2,5,8,10]])
```

In the first case, the two arrays have a first dimension that does not have the same size, we get an error. In the second case, we see that the two arrays have a common dimension (4). Therefore, the addition of the arr1 values is done for each value of the arr3 array. If, for example, we want to apply a transformation to an image that has been preferably transformed into the array, the dimensions of the images will be: (1000, 2000, 3). You can refer to the following paragraph for details on the characteristics of an image. Let's apply a transformation vector of dimension 3, and we will have:

```
In []: image.shape

Out []: (1000, 2000, 3)

In []: transf = np.array ([100, 255, 34])

transf.shape

Out []: (3,)

In []: new_image = image / transf

new_image.shape

Out []: (1000, 2000, 3)
```

The vector transf is applied to all the pixels, even if the dimensions do not correspond to lay only partially. We divide the first color by 100, the second by 255 and the third by 34. We will come back later to the treatment of images with NumPy.

Structured Arrays

The arrays we have used so far are arrays had only one type and no index other than the numerical index.

Structural arrays are arrays in which several types can cohabit with names associated with these "columns". These arrays are not used much in practice but it is important to know their existence. We can create this type of arrays using:

```
In []: array_struct = np.array ([[('Client A', 900, 'Paris'),

('Client B', 1200, 'Lyon')],

dtype = [('Clients', 'U10'),

('CA', 'int'), ('City', 'U10')])

In []: array_struct

Out []: array ([[('Client A', 900, 'Paris'), ('Client B', 1200,
'Lyon')],

dtype = [('Clients', '<U10'), ('CA', '<i4'), ('City', '<U10')])
```

We see here that the array is created as a series of tuples with the values of a line. Here we have three columns in our array and two lines. The part of type is very important because it allows defining the name and the type of a column.

We use as types <U10 which is a type of NumPy for character strings of less than 10 characters. To get a column in our array, just do:

```
In []: array_struct ['Clients']

Out []: array ([['Client A', 'Client B'],

dtype = '<U10')

To extract a value, we can use:

In []: array_struct ['CA'] [0]

Out []: 900
```

Nevertheless, this approach is not our preference. When we have data of different types with non-numerical indexes, we are interested in DataFrames and Pandas Series rather than structured arrays.

Operations and Functions

Numpy arrays, support arithmetic operations as expected. Here we will see some caveats of Broadcasting and built-in functions of the arrays.

Basic Operations

Same basic operations present in standard Python are also present in Numpy arrays. In this case, the operation between arrays of same shape results in another array.

Advanced Operations

There is also support for operations and transformations beyond the basics. Some advanced matrix operations are easily usable by functions in the linalg name space, attributes and methods of the object. For example, matrix product, determinant, inverse, etc.

CHAPTER - 6

PANDAS AND DATA MANIPULATION

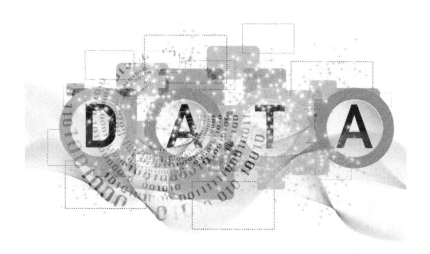

Pandas Installation

For installing Python Pandas, you need to go to the command line or terminal and then type "pip install pandas". Otherwise, in case you have anaconda installed on your computer, you may type in "conda install pandas". When this installation is finished go to the IDE, which may be PyCharm or Jupyter, and just import it with the command, "import pandas as pd." By moving forward for Python Pandas topic let us take a closer look at some of the operations it performs.

Basic Structures in Pandas

With some of this in mind, it is time for us to go through a few of the different things that we are able to do with the Pandas code. First, we need to look at the data structures. There are two of these data structures that we are able to work with, including the series and the DataFrame.

The first one here is the series. This is going to be similar to what we are able to work with when it comes to a one-dimensional array. It is able to go through and store data of any type. The values of a Pandas Series are going to be mutable, but you will find that the size of our series is going to be immutable, and we are not able to change them later.

The first element in this series is going to be given an index of 0. Then the last element that is going to be found in this kind of index is N-1 because N is going to be the total number of elements that we put into our series. To create one of our own Series in Pandas, we need to first go through the process of importing the package of Pandas through the insert command of Python. The code that we are able to use, including:

Import pandas as pd

Then we can go through and create one of our own Series. We are going to invoke the method of pd.Series() and then pass on the array. This is simple to work with. The code that we are able to use to help us work with this includes:

Series1 = pd.Series([1, 2, 3, 4])

We need to then work with the print statement in order to display the contents of the Series. You can see that when you run this one, you have two columns. The first one is going to be the first one with numbers starting from the index of 0 like we talked about before, and then the second one is going to be the different elements that we added to our series. The first column is going to denote the indexes for the elements.

However, you could end up with an error if you are working with the display Series. The major cause of this error is that the Pandas library is going to take some time to look for the amount of information that is displayed, this means that you need to provide the sys output information. You are also able to go through this with the help of a NumPy array like we talked about earlier. This is why we need to make sure that when we are working with the Pandas library, we also go through and install and use the NumPy library as well.

The second type of data structure that we are able to work with here will include the DataFrames. These are going to often come in as a table. It is going to be able to organize the data into columns and rows, which is going to turn it into a two-dimensional data structure. This means that we have the potential to have columns that are of a different type, and the size of the DataFrame that we want to work with will be mutable, and then it can be modified.

To help us to work with this and create one of our own, we need to either go through and start out a new one from scratch, or we are going to convert other data structures, like the arrays for NumPy into the DataFrame.

Pandas DataFrame

A Pandas DataFrame is probably the most used data structure offered by Pandas. A Pandas DataFrame is a rectangular table that contains an ordered collection of columns. A DataFrame column can each consist of different data types such as Booleans, strings, integers, etc. Unlike a series, a Pandas DataFrame has both rows and column indices. The best way to think of a Pandas as a DataFrame is like a spreadsheet document, or, on a more technical side, a dictionary of Pandas series sharing a unique index.

The most common way to create a Pandas DataFrame is by passing a python dictionary that contains equal length lists or a Numpy array to the DataFrame function.

```
In [7]: index = ['Barack Obama','Abraham Lincoln','John F Kennedy','George Washington','Franklin Roosevelt']
        data = {"Years":[8,4,2,8,12], "Number":[44,16,35,1,32]}

In [8]: dataFrame = pd.DataFrame(data, index=index)

In [9]: dataFrame
Out[9]:
                    Years   Number
    Barack Obama       8       44
    Abraham Lincoln    4       16
    John F Kennedy     2       35
    George Washington  8        1
    Franklin Roosevelt 12      32
```

First, we create a list containing the most popular presidents in the USA. Next, we create a dictionary containing their service years and the number which they served as president. Finally, we pass the data to the DataFrame function and their names as the index for the data. That results in a data frame containing the names of the presidents as the index, their service years and column 1 and their service number as column 2.

NOTE: Use Jupyter notebook while working with DataFrames as the formatting is friendly —HTML.

To retrieve a column in a Pandas DataFrame, we use either the dictionary notation —where we use the column name by using the attribute.

```
In [22]:  dataFrame['Presidents']

Out[22]:  0         Barack Obama
          1       Abraham Lincoln
          2        John F Kennedy
          3     George Washington
          4     Franklin Roosevelt
          Name: Presidents, dtype: object
```

```
In [24]:  dataFrame.Presidents

Out[24]:  0             Barack Obama
          1          Abraham Lincoln
          2           John F Kennedy
          3        George Washington
          4        Franklin Roosevelt
          Name: Presidents, dtype: object
```

Note that retrieving a column from a Pandas DataFrame produces a Pandas Series with its unique indices. This shows that a Pandas DataFrame consists of many Pandas Series. If you call the type function off the column, you will get a Pandas.core.series.Series data type.

```
In [25]:  type(dataFrame.Presidents)

Out[25]:  pandas.core.series.Series
```

We can also retrieve the rows of a Pandas DataFrame using a special loc attribute.

```
In [16]:  dataFrame.loc['Abraham Lincoln']

Out[16]:  Years      4
          Number     16
          Name: Abraham Lincoln, dtype: int64
```

NOTE: Depending on the method you use to execute the code used in the book, you might need to use the row number instead of the president's name and vice versa.

You can modify the Pandas dataframe columns by creating new ones and adding values to them. Let us add state column in our President's DataFrame as shown:

```
In [18]: dataFrame['State'] = ['Hawaii','Kentucky','Massachusetts','Virginia','New
```

```
In [19]: dataFrame
Out[19]:
```

	Years	Number	Country	State
Barack Obama	8	44	USA	Hawaii
Abraham Lincoln	4	16	USA	Kentucky
John F Kennedy	2	35	USA	Massachusetts
George Washington	8	1	USA	Virginia
Franklin Roosevelt	12	32	USA	New York

We pass the columns we want to add as a list followed by their corresponding values in respective order. Ensure to match the length of the DataFrame while assigning lists or arrays to a column to prevent occasions of missing data.

It is also important to note that assigning values to columns that do not exist will automatically create the column and assign to it the specified value.

To delete a column within a Pandas DataFrame, we use the del keyword, which is similar to how we delete a python dictionary. To illustrate column deletion, let us add a column called California and fill it with Boolean values – true if a president is from California and False if not.

```
In [21]:  dataFrame['california'] = dataFrame.State == 'California'

In [22]:  dataFrame
Out[22]:
```

	Years	Number	Country	State	california
Barack Obama	8	44	USA	Hawaii	False
Abraham Lincoln	4	16	USA	Kentucky	False
John F Kennedy	2	35	USA	Massachusetts	False
George Washington	8	1	USA	Virginia	False
Franklin Roosevelt	12	32	USA	New York	False

Using the del keyword, we can remove this column as shown below:

```
In [23]:  del dataFrame['california']

In [24]:  dataFrame
Out[24]:
```

	Years	Number	Country	State
Barack Obama	8	44	USA	Hawaii
Abraham Lincoln	4	16	USA	Kentucky
John F Kennedy	2	35	USA	Massachusetts
George Washington	8	1	USA	Virginia
Franklin Roosevelt	12	32	USA	New York

Now if we look at the existing columns within the DataFrame, we get four main columns as:

```
In [25]:  dataFrame.columns
Out[25]:  Index(['Years', 'Number', 'Country', 'State'], dtype='object')
```

Upon performing the del operation on the DataFrame, the returned column contains an actual view of the underlying data, which means that the operation occurs in-place, and any modifications undertaken on a section of the Pandas series also broadcasts to the original DataFrame.

You can copy a part of the Pandas array using the copy method. If a DataFrame does not have index and column name set, you can use the name attribute to accomplish this as shown below:

```
In [37]: dataFrame.index.name = ''; dataFrame.columns.name='Name'

In [38]: dataFrame
Out[38]:
```

Name	Years	Number	Country	State
Barack Obama	8	44	USA	Hawaii
Abraham Lincoln	4	16	USA	Kentucky
John F Kennedy	2	35	USA	Massachusetts
George Washington	8	1	USA	Virginia
Franklin Roosevelt	12	32	USA	New York

To get the values contained in a DataFrame, you can use the values attribute which returns a two-dimensional Numpy ndarrays, which is similar to the Pandas Series.

```
In [40]: dataFrame.values
Out[40]: array([[8, 44, 'USA', 'Hawaii'],
               [4, 16, 'USA', 'Kentucky'],
               [2, 35, 'USA', 'Massachusetts'],
               [8, 1, 'USA', 'Virginia'],
               [12, 32, 'USA', 'New York']], dtype=object)
```

In a scenario where the DataFrame's columns are of different data types, the data type of the values array is automatically set to accommodate all the columns in the DataFrame.

Now that one of the most common ways to create a Pandas has been talked about, let us look at some of the other types you can pass to the DataFrame function to create the DataFrame.

- A dictionary of dictionaries: Converts each inner dictionary to columns and merges the keys to form a row index.

- Two-dimensional Numpy array: Creates a DataFrame using the passed data. You can pass row and column labels but this optional.

```
In [51]: array = np.random.rand(5,5)

In [54]: new_dataFrame = pd.DataFrame(array)

In [55]: new_dataFrame
Out[55]:
```

	0	1	2	3	4
0	0.102508	0.985205	0.102353	0.851598	0.868762
1	0.070646	0.544700	0.461856	0.992644	0.549548
2	0.171221	0.953029	0.303306	0.606748	0.186475
3	0.661022	0.165850	0.575924	0.090192	0.708701
4	0.107004	0.267388	0.155782	0.381335	0.159966

- Numpy Masked Array

- Another Pandas DataFrame

- List of dictionaries

- List of series

- Numpy Structured array

Pandas Series

A Pandas series refers to a one-dimensional array-like object that contains a series of values —similar to a Numpy array and an associated array of labels called an index. We can create the simplest Pandas series using a Numpy array as shown below:

```
In [2]: array = np.arange(0,20)

In [3]: series = pd.Series(array)

In [4]: series

Out[4]: 0    0
        1    1
        2    2
        3    3
        4    4
        5    5
```

```
In [2]: array = np.arange(0,20)

In [3]: series = pd.Series(array)

In [4]: series

Out[4]: 0    0
        1    1
        2    2
        3    3
        4    4
        5    5
```

The above prints a Pandas series with all values from the Numpy array – generated using the arange function – and the index. The output above shows the index of the Pandas series on the Left and the actual values on the right.

As we did not specify the index we want used, a default index made up of integers 0 through N − 1 - where N is the length of the data - is used. Using a Pandas series values and index attributes, we can also get the array representation and index object of the Pandas series.

```
In [8]:  series.index
Out[8]:  RangeIndex(start=0, stop=20, step=1)

In [7]:  series.values  # use value attribute
Out[7]:  array([ 0,  1,  2,  3,  4,  5,  6,  7,  8,  9, 10, 11, 12, 13, 14, 15, 1
         6,
                17, 18, 19])
```

The best way is to create a Pandas series with index identifying each data point with a specified data label as shown:

```
In [9]:  indexed_Series = pd.Series([100,250,400,550,700], index=['OR','MI','MA','CA','VE'])

In [10]: indexed_Series
Out[10]: OR    100
         MI    250
         MA    400
         CA    550
         VE    700
         dtype: int64
```

For Pandas series, we can use the data labels in the index to select a single of a group of specific values.

```
In [12]:  indexed_Series['CA']
Out[12]:  550
```

This case is also true while selecting multiple elements using their respective indices.

```
In [13]:  indexed_Series[['CA','OR','MA']]
```

```
Out[13]:  CA      550
          OR      100
          MA      400
          dtype: int64
```

In the code above, the arguments ['CA', 'OR,' 'MA] interpret as a list of indices although it contains string type instead of integers.

It is also good to note that using Numpy operations or Numpy-like operations such as logical filtering, scalar multiplication, or mathematical functions call will not alter the index values:

```
In [15]:  np.exp(indexed_Series)
```

```
Out[15]:  OR        2.688117e+43
          MI        3.746455e+108
          MA        5.221470e+173
          CA        7.277212e+238
          VE        1.014232e+304
          dtype: float64
```

As you can see, doing this preserves the indices of the elements while it subjects the actual values to a mathematical exponential function.

You can also think of a Pandas series as a dictionary of fixed length where the indices represent the keys of dictionaries and the actual values are the array elements.

You can also pass a normal python dictionary to the Pandas Series function to create a series of elements.

```
In [19]: my_dict = {"OR": 100, "MI": 250, "MA": 400, "CA": 550, "VE": 700}
```

```
In [20]: pd.Series(my_dict)
Out[20]: OR      100
         MI      250
         MA      400
         CA      550
         VE      700
         dtype: int64
```

```
In [22]: indexed_Series.index = ['A','B','C','D','E']
```

```
In [23]: indexed_Series
Out[23]: A      100
         B      250
         C      400
         D      550
         E      700
         dtype: int64
```

A Pandas series assigns a value of NaN (Not a Number) to missing values. If a value is missing an index, the Pandas Series does not include it. We use the functions isnull and notnull to detect missing data.

Indexing, Selection, and Slicing

We can use the Pandas series indexing technique to select subsections of the Pandas DataFrame. Example:

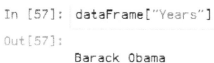

```
In [57]:  dataFrame["Years"]
Out[57]:
          Barack Obama              8
          Abraham Lincoln          4
          John F Kennedy           2
          George Washington        8
          Franklin Roosevelt      12
          Name: Years, dtype: int64
```

NOTE: This only selects the integral section of the DataFrame.

Slicing a Pandas data structure, however, behaves differently from the usual python slicing technique as the end value is inclusive.

CHAPTER - 7

DATA VISUALIZATION WITH PYTHON

Histogram Plotting

The histogram plots are normally utilized for summarizing the distribution of data samples. The x-axis of the plots represents discrete bins and intervals for their observations. For instance, the observations having values between 1 and 10 are split into 5 bins and the values [1,2} will be allocated to the first bins, next [3.4] are allocated to your 2nd bean and so on. Y-axis of the plot represents a frequency or a count of the number of observations in your data sets that belong to every bin. Typically, the data sample is transformed into the bar chart when each category of the x-axis is representing an interval of various observation values.

Histograms are also termed as density estimates. The density estimates provide a good impression of the data distribution. The whole idea is to represent the data density locally by counting the number of observations inside a sequence with consecutive intervals or bins. The histogram plots are created by calling the function hist() and passing it in an array or list that represents your data sample.

Box Plots

The whisker and box plots and they are also called box plots, in short, are generally utilized for summarizing the data sample distribution. The x-axes are utilized for representing the data samples while several box plots are drawn side by side on the x-axis in case they are required. Y-axis will represent the observation values. The box gets drawn for summarizing the middle half portion of data sets. This starts at the 25% stage and ends at eh 75% stage. Middle of this is the 50% stage and it is drawn by a line. There is a value called interquartile range or IQR. This is calculated as 1.5 times the difference between 25% and

75% values. The lines are called whiskers and they are drawn for the extension from both ends of your box with the IQR length for demonstration of an expected range of sensible values inside the distribution. Any observations out of the whiskers will be outliers and they are drawn by using small circles.

Box plots are graphical techniques used for the display of variable distribution. It helps in getting the location, spread, skewness, tile length, and outlying points. This box plot would be a graphical representation of your five number summaries. The box plots are drawn by placing a call to the boxplot() function and passing data samples as in the case of lists or arrays.

A scatter plot

The next type of plot that we are going to take some time to look at is a scatter plot. Even though to someone who is not looking that closely, it may seem like this is a random table with lots of dots, it is actually going to be a visualization tool of your data that is pretty powerful and can be used to show us a lot of information. Basically, this is going to be a data visualization tool that is two dimensional and will rely on dots to show us more of the values that have been obtained for two separate types of variables. One is going to be plotted using the X-axis, and the other one is going to be plotted along the y-axis.

Each of the dots that show up in the scatter plot is going to be important, and we need to use all of them to understand what is going on with the graphs and information that we are using. The information that comes with it is going to depend on what you are trying to learn. For example, if we are doing a scatterplot to show us the weight and height of children, we would see that the height of the child would be found on the x-axis, and then the weight is going to be measured using the y-axis.

With this understanding, we need to be able to look at the times when we would use these scatter plots, rather than relying on some of the other options that are out there. These kinds of scatter plots are going to be used any time that we would like to show there is a relationship that happens between our two variables.

A good way to look at these scatter plots is how they are sometimes called correlation plots, mainly because they are going to show us the correlation between two variables. Going back to the weight and height example that we talked about before, the chart wasn't just going to be a log of the weight and height of those children, but it is going to show us, in a visual form, the relationship between the weight and height. As we can guess, even before looking at the information in this case, when the weight increases, the height increases in children.

Now, while we often look at the linear forms of the scatter plots, it is important to note that not all of the relationships that you are going to encounter with this one are going to be linear. A good example of this one would be the average daily high temperature that is measured over seven years, showing a familiar parabolic relationship that happens between these variables where the temperature is going to be lower in the winter and the go back up again in the summer. And it is also possible for the data that you are using to have no kind of discernible relationship at all, which on its own can be interesting because it shows that all of your data doesn't have a correlation.

In addition to this, it is possible to have a few common extensions that go with the scatter plots. Often these are going to include some kind of trendline that helps us to see the relationship a bit better and can give us kind of the median when it comes to the chosen information. We may also find that the color, the shape, and the size of the dot could represent a third, and sometimes even a fourth, variable on the information. You could change up the different dots in the height and weight category into those who are male and those who are female, to see the differences that could occur between the two genders when it comes to their height and weight.

The scatter plots can be a useful tool when it is time for us to look at the relationship that forms between two variables, but you have to have a good idea of how you can use these, and how you can interpret them in the proper manner. With this in mind, the code below is going to be used to help you create one of these scatter plots on your own system using the data that you already have available:

```
import numpy as np

import matplotlib.pyplot as plt

import matplotlib.cbook as cbook

# Load a numpy record array from yahoo csv data with fields date, open, close,

# volume, adj_close from the mpl-data/example directory. The record array

# stores the date as an np.datetime64 with a day unit ('D') in the date column.

with cbook.get_sample_data('goog.npz') as datafile:
```

```
price_data =
np.load(datafile)['price_data'].view(np.recarray)
```

```
price_data = price_data[-250:] # get the most recent 250
trading days

delta1 = np.diff(price_data.adj_close) /
price_data.adj_close[:-1]

# Marker size in units of points^2

volume = (15 * price_data.volume[:-2] /
price_data.volume[0])**2

close = 0.003 * price_data.close[:-2] / 0.003 *
price_data.open[:-2]

fig, ax = plt.subplots()

ax.scatter(delta1[:-1], delta1[1:], c=close, s=volume,
alpha=0.5)

ax.set_xlabel(r'$\Delta_i$', fontsize=15)

ax.set_ylabel(r'$\Delta_{i+1}$', fontsize=15)

ax.set_title('Volume and percent change')

ax.grid(True)

fig.tight_layout()

plt.show()
```

Visualisation with Seaborn

It is another Python data visualization library that is based on the popular one Matplotlib. Seaborn gives you a high level interface for the creation of attractive graphs. This library has plenty to offer. It is possible to create graphs in one line that will take several tens of lines for the Matplotlib. The standard designs used here are very useful and it also comes with a terrific interface for working with pandas. This library may be imported by typing:

import seaborn as sns

Heatmap

It is another graphical data representation where the independent values contained within a matrix are represented in the form of colors. The Heatmaps are ideal for the exploration of co-relations of features for the dataset. For acquiring the co-relations of the features within a data set you can call

```
<dataset>.corr()
```

It is a method used by Pandas data frame. It will provide you a co-relation matrix. You might utilize either Seaborn or Matplotlib for the creation of Heatmaps.

CHAPTER - 8

MACHINE LEARNING WITH PYTHON

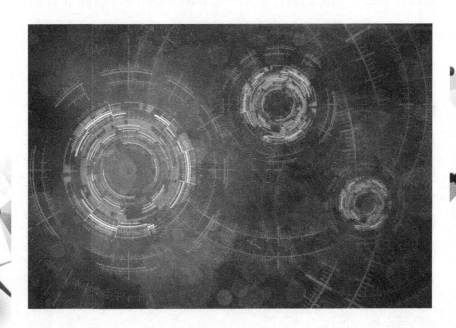

What is Machine Learning?

The first thing that we need to take a look at here is the basics of machine learning. This is going to be one of the techniques that we can use with data analytics that will help teach a computer how to learn and react on their own, without the interaction of the programmer. Many of the actions that we will train the system to do will be similar to actions that already come naturally to humans, such as learning from experience.

The algorithms that come with machine learning are going to be able to use computational methods in order to learn information right from the data, without having to rely on an equation that is predetermined as its model. The algorithms are going to adaptively improve some of their own performance as the number of samples that we will use for learning will increase.

There are a lot of instances where we are able to use machine learning. With the rise in big data that is available for all industries to use, We will find that machine learning is going to become one of the big techniques that are used to solve a ton of problems in many areas, including the following:

1. Computational finance: This is going to include algorithmic trading, credit scoring, and fraud detection.

2. Computer vision and other parts of image processing. This can be used in some different parts like object detection, motion detection, and face recognition.

3. Computational biology. This is going to be used for a lot of different parts, including DNA sequencing, drug discovery, and tumor detection.

4. Energy production. This can be used to help with a few different actions like load forecasting and to help predict what the prices will be.

5. Manufacturing, aerospace, and automotive options. This is going to be a great technique to work with when it comes to helping with many parts, including predictive maintenance.

6. Natural language processing: This is going to be the way that we can use machine learning to help with applications of voice recognition.

Machine learning and the algorithms that they control are going to work by finding some natural patterns in the data that you can use, including using it in a manner that will help us to make some better predictions and decisions along the way. They are going to be used on a daily basis by businesses and a lot of different companies in order to make lots of critical decisions.

For example, medical facilities can use this to help them to help diagnose patients. And we will find that there are a lot of media sites that will rely on machine learning in order to sift through the potential of millions of options in order to give recommendations to the users. Retailers can use this as a way to gain some insight into the purchasing behavior of their customers along the way.

There are many reasons that your business is able to consider using machine learning. For example, it is going to be useful if you are working with a task that is complex or one that is going to involve a larger amount of data and a ton of variables, but there isn't an equation or a formula that is out there right now to handle it. For example, some of the times when we want to work with machine learning include:

1. Equations and rules that are hand-written and too complex to work with. This could include some options like speech recognition and face recognition.

2. When you find that the rules that are going to change all of the time. This could be seen in actions lie fraud detection from a large number of transactional records.

3. When you find that the nature of your data is going to change on a constant basis, and the program has to be able to adapt along the way. This could be seen when we work with predicting the trends during shopping when doing energy demand forecasting and even automated trading, to name a few.

As you can see, there are a lot of different things that we are able to do when it comes to machine learning, and pretty much any industry is going to be able to benefit from working with this for their own needs. Machine learning is more complex, but we are able to combine it together with Python in order to get some amazing results in the process and to ensure that our data analysis is going to work the way that we want.

Decision trees and Random forests

Decision trees: A decision tree algorithm tries to classify the elements by identifying questions concerning their attributes that will assist decide of which class to place them. Each node inside the tree is a question, with branches that lead to more questions about the articles, and the leaves as the final classifications.

Use cases for decision trees can include the construction of knowledge management platforms for customer service, price predictions, and product planning.

An insurance agency could utilize a decision tree when it requires data about the sort of protection items and the excellent changes dependent on possible hazard, says Ray Johnson, boss information researcher at business and innovation counseling firm SPR. Utilizing area information overlaid with climate related misfortune information, you can make hazard classes dependent on claims made and cost sums. It would then be able to assess new models of fence against models to give a hazard class and a potential monetary effect, the official said.

Random Forests: A decision tree must be prepared to give precise outcomes, the irregular timberland calculation takes a lot of irregular choice trees that base their choices on various arrangements of attributes and permit them to cast a ballot in the most well-known request.

Random forests are simply flexible devices for discovering connections in data sets and quick to train, says Epstein. For example, unsolicited bulk mail has been a problem for a long time, not only for users but also for Internet service providers that have to manage the increased load on servers. In response to this problem, automated methods have been developed to filter spam from standard email, using random forests to quickly and accurately identify unwanted emails, the executive said.

Other uses of random forests include the identification of disease by analyzing the patient's medical records, detecting bank fraud, predicting the volume of calls in the call centers and predicting gains or losses through the Purchase of a particular stock.

SciKit-Learn

This is a fundamental tool used in data-mining and data analysis related tasks. This is an open-source tool and licensed under BSD. This tool can be accessed or reused in different contexts. SciKit has been developed on top of

NumPy, Matplotlib, and SciPy. The tool is utilized for classification, regression, and clustering and managing spam, image recognition, stock pricing, drug response, and customer segmentation, etc. The tool also permits model selection, dimensionality reduction, and pre-processing.

Linear Regression

The word "linearity" in algebra implies a linear connection between two or more variables. If we draw this connection in a two-dimensional space (amongst two variables), we get a conservative line.

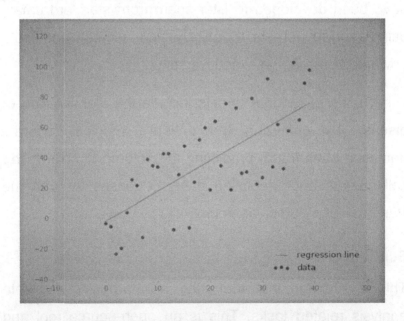

Linear regression completes the duty to foresee a dependent variable rate (y) built on a certain independent variable (x). So, this regression method finds out a linear connection between x (input) in addition to y (output). Thus, they term it the Linear Regression. If we plot the dependent and independent variable (y and x) on their axis, linear regression gives us a conventional line that fits the information plugs as revealed in the picture below. We then recognize that the equation of a conventional line is essential.

The equation of the overhead line is:

Y= mx + b

Where b is the advert and m are the hills of the line. So, essentially, the linear regression algorithm gives us the greatest ideal rate for the advert and the hill (in two magnitudes). Although the y and x variables produce the result, they are the data structures and cannot be altered. The figures that we can switch are the advert(b) and hill(m). There can be numerous conventional lines relying upon the figures of the advert and the figures of the hill. Essentially, what the linear regression algorithm ensures is it fits numerous lines on the data points and yields the line that results in the slightest mistake.

This similar idea can be stretched to cases where there are additional variables. This is termed numerous linear regressions. For example, think about a situation where you must guess the price of the house built upon its extent, the number of bedrooms, the regular income of the people in the area, the oldness of the house, and so on. In this situation, the dependent variable (target variable) is reliant on numerous independent variables. A regression model including numerous variables can be signified as:

y = b0 + m1b1 + m2b2 + m3b3 + ... mnbn

This is the comparison of a hyperplane. Recall that a linear regression model in two magnitudes is a straight line; in three magnitudes it is a plane, and in additional magnitudes, a hyperplane.

Support Vector Machines (SVM)

A managed algorithm used for machine learning which can mutually be employed for regression or classification challenges is Support Vector Machines. Nevertheless, it is typically employed in classification complications. In this algorithm, we design each data entry as a point in n-dimensional space (where n is many structures you have) with the rate of each feature being the rate of a coordinate. Then, we complete the classification by finding the hyper-plane that distinguishes the two classes very well.

Look at the image below:

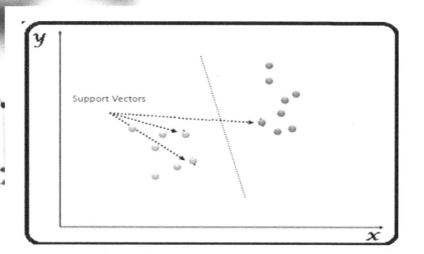

Support Vectors are the coordinates of separate thoughts. Support Vector Machine is a borderline that best isolates the two classes (hyper-plane/ line).

K-means Clustering

The 2000 and 2004 Constitutional determinations in the United States were closed. The highest percentage received by any runner from a general ballot was 50.7% and the lowest was 47.9%. If a proportion of the electorates were to have their sides swapped, the result of the determination would have been dissimilar. There are small clusters of electorates who, when appropriately enticed, will change sides. These clusters may not be gigantic, but with such close competitions, they might be big enough to change the result of the determination. By what means do you find these clusters of individuals? By what means do you petition them with an inadequate budget? To do this, you can employ clustering.

Let us recognize how it is done.

- First, you gather data on individuals either with or without their permission: any kind of data that might give an approximate clue about what is vital to them and what will affect how they vote.
- Then you set this data into a clustering algorithm.
- Next, for each group (it would be very nifty to select the principal one first), you create a letter that will appeal to these electorates.
- Lastly, you send the campaign and measure to see if it's employed.

Clustering is a category of unsupervised learning that routinely makes clusters of comparable groups. It is like an involuntary classification. You can cluster nearly everything, and the more comparable the objects are in the cluster, the enhanced the clusters are.

Naïve Bayes

The Naïve Bayes algorithm is a good choice to go with when you want to do a bit of exploration with the data in the beginning. Maybe you want to see what the best way is to split up the data that you have, or you are not yet certain about what kind of algorithm is going to be the best one for you to focus your attention on yet. In some cases, you may need to show some of the data and some of the information that you have ahead of time, right after collecting it, to those who want to see what is going on, but may not understand all of the more technical aspects that come with it.

This is where the Naïve Bayes algorithm is going to come into play and can really help us. With this option, we are able to take a good exploration of the data that we have, and then determine the best steps to take after. Sometimes this helps us to choose which of the other algorithms are the best ones for us to go with. And other times, it may be a good way to create a beginner's model so that we can show this off before being able to finish all of the work for the final project.

The Naïve Bayes algorithm is usually not going to be the first choice that we make when it is time to handle some of our data, and we will usually go through and make a few other adjustments to the process as well and finish off with another kind of algorithm. But it is definitely a good algorithm to go with because it adds in a lot of the different parts that you need to get a good idea about what the data contains, and what else we are able to do with it along the way.

CHAPTER - 9

APPLICATIONS OF MACHINE LEARNING

Deep Learning

The first topic that we need to dive into here is what deep learning is all about. Deep learning is considered a function that comes with artificial intelligence, one that is able to imitate, as closely as possible, some of the workings we see in the human brain when it comes to creating patterns and processing complex data to use with decision making. Basically, we can use the parts of deep learning to help us take our machine or our system and teach it how to think through things the same way that a human can, although at a faster and more efficient rate.

So, to get a better idea of how this is going to benefit us, we first need to take a look at how we can work with deep learning. The process of deep learning has really evolved a lot in the past few years, going hand in hand with a lot of the things we have seen in the digital era. This time period has really brought about so much data, data that comes in so many forms. In particular, this data is known as big data, and we will be able to draw it out of a lot of different areas such as e-commerce platforms, search engines, social media, and more.

If a company uses some of the algorithms that come with machine learning, they will be able to actually use all of the information that they are collecting. They can use it to recommend products for their customers, to really work on making predictions and finding patterns with the information so they can really run their business the way that they would like.

You will notice though that this unstructured data is going to be pretty large, and for an employee to go through this information and get the relevant parts from it, it would take so long the information would no longer be relevant and useful. And by the time they did, the information would be old, and the world would have already moved on and presented different information. But many companies still realized the potential that they could learn from all of this information, even if it is pretty large, and many are looking at the different ways that various systems of AI can help them get through this information and gain the insights that they need.

Look at how deep learning is going to work. Deep learning has evolved at the same time and often at the same pace as we see with the digital era. This is an era that has seen a big explosion of data in all forms, and from every region of the world. This is a lot of data, and it is there to help businesses make informed decisions that weren't possible in the past.

Think about all of the information that you already have at your fingertips, and you may not even realize that it is there. Before you even decide to start working with big data, you already know that if you need to look up something, you can head to your favorite search engine and it will all be there. Our digital era is bringing out a ton of new information and data, and the smart companies, the ones who would like to get ahead, are the ones who not only gather all of that data, but who learn how to use it.

This data, which is often called big data, is drawn from a variety of sources depending on what the business is trying to accomplish. These can come from places like e-commerce platforms, search engines, online cinemas, search engines, and more. The enormous amount of data that fits into the category of big data is going to be readily accessible to anyone who wants it, and it is possible to share it through a lot of different applications like cloud computing.

However, this data, which is normally going to come to us in a form that is unstructured, is so vast that if a person manually went through all of it, it may take decades to extract out the information that is relevant to what they need. Companies realize this, and they now that there is a lot of potential that can be found in all of that data that they have collected. And this is why creating and adapting artificial intelligence systems with automated support is something that many of them have started to focus their attention on.

Natural Language Processing

Have you noticed that more and more companies are putting a bot widget on their site? Chatbots are everywhere today. And of Natural Language Processing (NLP) and Natural Language Understanding (NLU) technologies. The potential of NLP and NLU seems limitless. Now everyone understands that we are only at the beginning of a long journey.

Titans in the IT industry are creating dedicated research departments to explore this area. Intel did not stand aside. Recently, Intel AI Lab released a product called NLP Architect. This is an open source library designed to serve as the basis for further research and collaboration of developers from around the world.

NLP Architect

A team of NLP researchers and developers from Intel AI Lab is studying the current architecture of deep neural networks and methods for processing and understanding text. The result of their work was a set of tools that are interesting from both a theoretical and an applied point of view.

Here's what the current version of NLP Architect has:

- Models that extract the linguistic characteristics of text: for example, a parser (BIST) and an algorithm for extracting nouns (noun phrases);

- State-of-the-art models for understanding the language: for example, determination of user intent (intent extraction), recognition of named entities (named entity recognition, NER);

- Modules for semantic analysis: for example, collocations, the most probable meaning of a word, vector representations of named groups (NP2V);

- Building blocks for creating conversational intelligence: for example, the basis for creating chatbots, including a dialogue support system, a sequence analyzer (sequence chunker), a system for determining the user's intent;

- Examples of using deep end-to-end neural networks with a new architecture: for example, question-answer systems, text reading systems (machine reading comprehension).

- For all of the above models, there are examples of learning and prediction processes. Moreover, the Intel team added scripts to solve typical tasks that arise when implementing such models - pipelines for data processing and utilities that are often used in NLP.

The library consists of separate modules, which simplifies integration. A general view of the NLP Architect framework is shown in the diagram below.

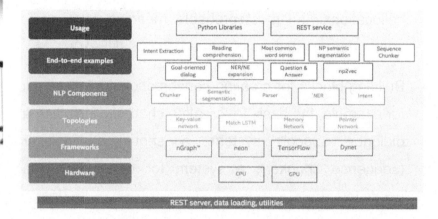

Usage		Python Libraries		REST service		
End-to-end examples	Intent Extraction	Reading comprehension	Most common word sense	NP semantic segmentation	Sequence Chunker	
	Goal-oriented dialog	NER/NE expansion	Question & Answer	np2vec		
NLP Components	Chunker	Semantic segmentation	Parser	NER	Intent	
Topologies	Key-value network	Match LSTM	Memory Network	Pointer Network		
Frameworks	nGraph™	neon	TensorFlow	Dynet		
Hardware		CPU	GPU			

REST server, data loading, utilities

NLP Architect Framework

Components for NLP / NLU

Offer analyzer. Analysis of sentences (sequence chunking) is one of the basic tasks of word processing, which consists in dividing sentences into syntactically related parts. For example, a sentence

"Little Sasha walked along the highway" can be divided into four parts: the nouns "Little Sasha" and "highway", the verb group "walked" and the prepositional group "by".

The analyzer of sentences from NLP Architect can build suitable neural network architecture for different types of input data: tokens, labels of parts of speech, vector representations, symbolic signs.

Semantic segmentation of noun groups. A noun phrase consists of the main member - a noun or pronoun - and several dependent qualifying members. To simplify, you can divide nouns into two types:

- With descriptive structure: dependent members do not significantly affect the semantics of the main member (for example, "sea water");

- With collocation structure: dependent members significantly change the meaning of the main term (for example, "guinea pig").

To determine the type of name group, a multilayer perceptron is trained. This model is used in the semantic sentence segmentation algorithm. As a result of her work, nouns of the first type break up into several semantic elements, and nouns of the second type remain unified.

The parser performs grammar analysis of sentences, examining the relationship between words in sentences and highlighting things like direct additions and predicates. NLP Architect includes a graph-based dependency parser that uses BiLSTM to extract features.

The Named Entity Recognizer (NER) identifies certain words or combinations of words in a text that belong to a certain class of interest to us. Examples of entities include names, numbers, places, currencies, dates, organizations.

Sometimes entities can be quite easily distinguished with the help of such features as the form of words, the presence of a word in a certain dictionary, part of speech. However, quite often these signs are not known to us or even exist. In such cases, in order to determine whether a word or phrase is an entity, it is necessary to analyze its context.

The model for NER in NLP Architect is based on a bidirectional LSTM network and CRF classifier. A high-level review of the model is presented below.

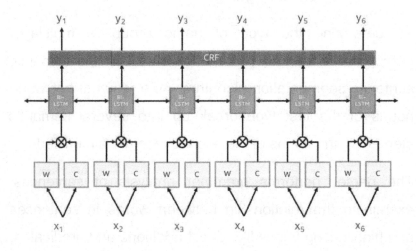

High Level Review of the NER Model

The user intent determination algorithm solves the problem of understanding the language. Its purpose is to understand what kind of action is discussed in the text, and to identify all parties involved. For example, for a sentence

"Siri, please remind me to pick up things from the laundry on the way home."

The algorithm determines the action ("remind"), who should perform this action ("Siri"), who asks to perform this action ("I") and the object of the action ("pick up things from the laundry").

The analyzer of the meaning of the word. The algorithm receives a word at the input and returns all the meanings of this word, as well as numbers characterizing the prevalence of each of the meanings in the language.

NLP Architect Visualizer

The library includes a small web server - NLP Architect Server. It makes it easy to test the performance of different NLP Architect models. Among other things, the server has visualizers, which are pretty nice diagrams that demonstrate the operation of the models. Currently, two services support visualization - a parser and a recognizer of named entities. In addition, there is a template with which the user can add visualization for other services.

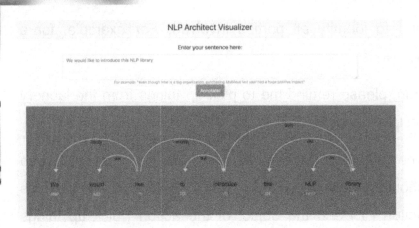

NLP Architect is an open and flexible library with algorithms for word processing, which makes it possible for developers from all over the world to interact. The Intel team continues to add the results of its research to the library so that anyone can take advantage of what they have done and improved.

To get started, just download the code from the Github repository and follow the installation instructions. Here you can find comprehensive documentation for all the main modules and ready-made models.

In future releases, Intel AI Lab plans to demonstrate the benefits of creating text analysis algorithms using the latest deep learning technologies, and include methods for extracting text tonality, analyzing topics and trends, expanding specialized vocabulary, and extracting relationships in the library. In addition, Intel experts are exploring teaching methods without teacher and partial training, with which you can create new interpretable models for understanding and analyzing text that can adapt to new areas of knowledge.

Neural Network

The first type of network we are going to look at is the "normal" type of neural network. These neural networks are going to fit into the category of unsupervised machine learning because they are able to work on their own and provide us with some great results in the process. Neural networks are a great option to work within machine learning because they are set up to catch onto any pattern or trend that is found in a set of data. This can be done through a variety of levels, and in a way that is going to be much faster and more effective than a human going through and doing the work manually.

When we work with a neural network, each of the layers that we will focus on are responsible for spending time in that layer, seeing if they are able to find a pattern or trend inside the image, or through the data, that it looks at. Once it has found a trend or a pattern, it is going to start its process for entering into the next layer. This process is going to continue, with the network finding a new pattern or trend, and then going on to the next level, until it reaches a place where there are no more trends or patterns to find.

This process can end up with a lot of different layers, one over the top of the others again and again, until you have been able to see the whole thing that comes in the image. When the algorithm is created, and the program can make a good prediction based on what is in the image or in the data that you present, then you know that it has all been set up properly.

Before we move on though, we have to remember that there are a few parts that will start to occur at this point, based on how you set up the program to work. If the algorithm was able to read through all of the layers and the steps above, and it had success with reading through the different layers, then it is able to make a good prediction for you. If the algorithm is accurate with the prediction that it made, then the neurons that come with this algorithm will strengthen and become faster and more efficient at their job overall.

Keep in mind that the more times that the algorithm is able to provide the right answer during this process, the more efficient it will become when you try to use it another time as well. The neurons get stronger, and you will see that the answers come faster and are more accurate overall.

Now, if you haven't been able to work with machine learning and deep learning in the past, it may seem like these neural networks would be impossible to actually see happen. But a closer examination of these algorithms can help us to see better how they work and why they can be so important to this process. For the example that we are going to work with, let's say that we have a goal to make a program that can take the image we present, and then, by going through the different layers, the program is able to recognize that the image in that picture is actually a car.

If we have created the neural network in the proper manner, then it is able to take a look at the image that we use and make a good prediction that it sees a car in the picture. The program will then be able to come up with this prediction based on any features and parts that it already knows comes with a car. This could include things like the color, the license plate, the door placement, where the headlights are, and more.

When we take a look at coding with some of the traditional methods, whether they are Python methods or not, this is something that you may be able to do, but it takes way too long and is not the best option to work with. It can take a lot of coding and really just confuse up the whole process. But with these neural networks, you will be able to write out the codes to get this kind of network done in no time.

To get the neural network algorithm to work the way that you want, you have to provide the system with a good and clear image of a car. The network can then take a look at that picture and start going through some of the layers that it needs to work with to see the picture. So, the system will be able to go through the first layer, which may include something like the outside edges of the car. When it was done with this, the network would continue on from one layer to the next, going through however many layers it takes to complete the process and provide us with a good prediction. Sometimes this is just a few layers, but the more layers this program can go through, the more likely it will provide an accurate prediction in the end.

Depending on the situation or the project that you want to work with, there is the potential for adding in many different layers. The good news with this one is that the more details and the more layers that a neural network can find, the more accurately it can predict what object is in front of it, and even what kind of car it is looking at.

As the neural network goes through this process, and it shows a result that is accurate when identifying the car model, it is actually able to learn from that lesson, similar to what we see with the human brain. The neural network is set up in a way to remember the patterns and the different characteristics that it saw in the car model, and con store onto that information to use at another time if it encounters another car that is the same again. So, if you present, at a later time, another image with that same car model in it, then the neural network can make a prediction on that image fairly quickly.

There are several options that you can choose to use this kind of system for, but remember that each time you make a neural network, it is only able to handle one task at a time. you can make a neural network that handles facial recognition for example, and one that can find pictures that we need in a search engine, but you can't make one neural network do all of the tasks that you want. You may have to split it up and make a few networks to see this happen.

For example, there is often a lot of use for neural networks when it comes to creating software that can recognize faces. All of the information that you need to create this kind of network would not be available ahead of time, so the neural network will be able to learn along the way and get better with recognizing the faces that it sees in video or images. This is also a method that can be effective when you would like to get it to recognize different animals or recognize a specific item in other images or videos as well.

To help us out here, we need to take a look at some of the advantages that can come with this kind of model with machine learning. One of the advantages that a lot of programmers like with this one is that you can work with this algorithm without having to be in total control over the statistics of the algorithm. Even if you are not working with statistics all of the time, or you are not really familiar with how to use them, you will see that these networks can be used without those statistics, still that if there is any relationship, no matter how complex it is, is inside the information, then it is going to show up when you run the network.

The nice thing with this one is that the relationships inside your data can be found, whether the variables are dependent or independent, and even if you are working with variables that do not follow a linear path. This is good information for those who are just getting started with machine learning because it ensures that we can get a better understanding of how the data relates to each other, and some of the insights that you want to work with, no matter what variables you are working with.

With this in mind, we have to remember that there are still times when we will not use a neural network, and it will not be the solution to every problem that we want to handle in deep learning. One of the bigger issues that come with these neural network algorithms, and why some programmers decide to not use this is that the computing costs are going to be kind of high.

This is an algorithm that is pretty in-depth, and because of this, the computing costs are going to be a bit higher than what we find with some of the other options out there. and for some businesses, and even on some of the projects that you want to do with deep learning, this computation cost will just be too high. It will take on too much power, too much money, and often too much time. For some of the projects that you want to take on, the neural networks will be a great addition to your arsenal with deep learning, and other times, you may want to go another route.

Neural networks are a great option to work with when it is time to expand out your work and when you would like to create a program that can handle some more complex activities. With the right steps here, and with some time to train the neural network, you will find that the neural network is a great way to handle your data and find the trends and predictions that you want.

Clustering

Clustering algorithms use techniques such as K-means, mean-shift, or expectation-maximation to group data points based on shared or related characteristics, this is an unsupervised learning method that can be applied to the classification problems.

Clustering technique is particularly useful when you need to segment or categorize, Schatsky notes. Examples include segmenting customers by different characteristics to assign marketing campaigns better, recommending news articles to confident readers, and effective law enforcement.

The clustering is likewise dynamic for discovering clusters in complex informational indexes that may not be evident to the natural eye. Examples range from the categorization of similar documents in a database to the identification of critical crime points in crime reports, says Epstein.

CONCLUSION

This is the end of the book. The next milestone is to make the best use of your new-found wisdom of Python programming, data science, data analysis, and machine learning that have resulted in the birth of the powerhouse, which is the "Silicon Valley." So many companies, that span a lot of different industries, are able to benefit when they work with data analysis. This allows them to get a lot of the power and control that they want for their respective industries and will ensure that they will be able to really impress their customers and get some good results in the process. Learning how to use a data analysis is going to change the game in how you do business, as long as it is used in the proper manner.

This guidebook has been organized well to explore what data analysis is all about, and how we are able to use this for our benefits as well. There are a lot of business tools out there, but data analysis is designed to help us focus on finding the hidden patterns and insights that are in our data, making it easier to base our decisions on data, rather

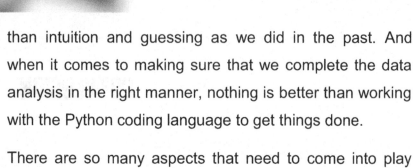

than intuition and guessing as we did in the past. And when it comes to making sure that we complete the data analysis in the right manner, nothing is better than working with the Python coding language to get things done.

There are so many aspects that need to come into play when we are working with our own data analysis, and it is important that we take the time to learn how these works, and how to put it all together. And that is exactly what we will do in this guidebook. When you are ready to learn more about Python data analysis, and all of the different parts that come together to help us with understanding our data and how to run our business, make sure to recheck this guide to help you.

You would also develop skills in loading and exporting dataset from and to Python environments. You would also acquire skills in analysis and processing datasets using both libraries NumPy and Pandas by handling missing data and exploring datasets. You would develop skill in visualizing data using different type of graphs as well by mastering the functionalities of the matplotlib library.

Overall this book provides a guide on using these handy libraries in data analysis. Once you have acquired these skills and know the functionalities of the NumPy, Pandas and Matplotlib libraries, you will be able to analyze any data you have in hand using Python. You also develop more advanced skills to handle complex datasets.

Now that you have finished reading this book and mastered the use of Python programming, you are all set to start developing your own Python based machine learning model as well as performing big data analysis using all the open sources readily available and explicitly described in this book. You can position yourself to use your deep knowledge and understanding of all the cutting edge technologies obtained from this book to contribute to the growth of any company and land yourself a new high paying and rewarding job!

Made in the USA
Coppell, TX
20 March 2024

30341335R00066